SEVEN STRING QUARTETS

FRÉDÉRIC FORTE

SEVEN STRING QUARTETS

TRANSLATION
Matthew B. Smith

La Presse
IOWA CITY & PARIS 2014

Seven String Quartets was first published as part of *Discographie,*
Éditions de l'Attente © 2002
Translation copyright © 2014 Matthew B. Smith

Published in the United States by La Presse,
an imprint of Fence Books

La Presse/Fence Books are distributed by Consortium
www.cbsd.com
www.lapressepoetry.com

Library of Congress Control Number 2014932439
Frédéric Forte
Seven String Quartets by Frédéric Forte,
translated by Matthew B. Smith
p.   cm.

ISBN 978-1-934200-81-0

1. French poetry. 2. Poetry. 3. Contemporary translation.

First Edition
10 9 8 7 6 5 4 3 2 1

We warmly thank the editors of Éditions de l'Attente for
generously allowing us to publish this translation of the work.
You can find out more about the wonderful collection of contemporary
French writing that they publish through their website at
www.editionsdelattente.com

SEVEN STRING QUARTETS

STRING QUARTET #1

I (*Forms*)

Forms seated on a green
bench dog pissing on a street
lamp yellow cloud
of smoke

Forms getting fresh air flag
stones ring and wobble hands
turning cold cloud
scarves

Forms at the windows eyes
fixed on passersby purr
of heaters and on the air
        a dull record

                        Forms on side streets back-
                        lit against sketchy stretch
                        silhouette dash or solemn
                                old man

II (*Stones*)

The second one throws a stone
and waits and waits another
stone and returns the stone
to the sender

The first one throws a stone
and waits then throws another
stone and another and an
other stone

The third one throws no
stone throws no stone
back to the sender who never
          threw one

                              The fourth one throws none
                              and waits for a stone from
                              the sender who may throw
                                    the next stone

III (*News briefs*)

No point look no point
to do nothing tries what
who knows knows
what's best

Goes by doesn't look
goes by self involved
who knows his way
doesn't linger

In tatters sad soul
less romantic can't
hold back his vomit and
          falls flat

                              Cut short long mouth
                              to mouth short of breath
                              with his hand takes
                                        his pulse

IV *(Character Traits)*

Hands pale split
shaking the fence
to be seen
Clear nonchalance   at last
pure brain adrift
cigarette holder in step
with the time

Tender lonesome soul
passionately withdrawn
smiling sweetly at
        every onlooker

                Eternal enemy of
                the front his boots
                strewn under the wreck
                        of the table

V (*Garage*)

In the clutter there's
always the rich text
ure of disorder is
intended

He fumbles with
a lit match sees sharp
objects ends up
finding

At the doorstep
imagines clearly the
location of each thing
in its place

Arm in elbow grease
regular sludge for who
escapes the daily grind of
the hands-on

VI (*Stages*)

On top the tiptop
light weight the light dancer
down to her shin
splints

A sprint finish nice
straight line on the foresight
released rolling its mechanical
shoulders

Alone in its bubble
perfect escape
miles unravel chasing
            the white line

                    Old fox focused and
                    resourceful does his
                    job and kills
                            in the 100m

STRING QUARTET #2

I (*Calm*)

Calm waterline
clear unbroken line
leaving the port few
waves

Few waves leaving
the port calm water
line clear unbroken
line

Clear leaving the port
line unbroken line
few waves of calm
   water

         The port line clear
         leaving the calm water
         unbroken waves few
            lines

II (*Merry-go-round*)

Tonight the ginger horse
will take off without
its bucket of water its
ration of oats

Kid on the saddle
is the white horse's
pride king of
the show

Gray dappled horse
despairs one day
of hearing hoofs
        beat the road

                Monsieur Loyal makes
                the horses go round if
                one escapes he is
                        lost

III (*Immobile*)

Blow corner
of the wall no plan
nor a bug horn
of wind

Horn blow corner
of the wall no plan
nor a bug horn
of wind

Horn blow
of the wall no plan
nor a bug horn
    of wind

Horn blow corner
of the wall no plan
nor a bug horn
    of wind

STRING QUARTET #3

(You)

Rest my eyes rest
my hands then close
them and do nothing
but this

You in your dress and your
coal black eyes me caught
between staring and
undressing you

Look at you look at you
listen to you and tell you
fall quiet and look at you
some more

And you so close your
eyes on these lines I'm
blushing watching you
read

STRING QUARTET #4

I (*Nocturnal*)

It traps light and
goes for the most
reckless or the most
oblivious

From unknown heights
we guess at the stars
each one a shot
in the dark

We swim in clear water
stripped bare and fully
exposed it's almost
                unthinkable
                                  The time of insects of
                                  roots of obstacles
                                  adept and bent on
                                              our aim

II (*Trio*)

Words follow words
nothing left to explain
to those who can't
keep up

(is this the
pause this
parenthetical
moment)

The trio is so dark why
this dismemberment
why keep up
    the show

                    Unfilled blank space
                    counters mute
                    resistance like blind
                          wall

III (*Savage*)

Sudden big blast
you must be the most
dense the most trivial
the most savage

Sudden big blast
you must be the most
dense the most trivial
the most savage

~~Sudden big blast~~
~~you must be the most~~
dense the most trivial
~~the most savage~~

Sudden big blast
~~you must be the most~~
~~dense the most trivial~~
~~the most savage~~

STRING QUARTET #5

I (*Cold*)

The victims disappear
behind the arras at the
well bottom poison is
banned

No shouts no soul
spilling no shaking
in a steady and
careful voice

In the halls they pass
each other in silence
with no visible sign
of thought

Voluntary withdrawal
from life's affairs to
a single cell form of
asceticism

II (*Red*)

The fruit rotting
on its mat of leaves
gives heat to
the invisible

A new horizon
proves itself every
day makes its offer
public

Decorative paper like
a firefly's carapace
tints the tables on
    Bastille Day

The embers of
the unsaid claim
a small space for
    speech

III (*Lift*)

The act of anvil
lifting is an act
which requires some
strength

To lift an anvil
takes strength to lift
an anvil or any other
object

To lift any other
object requires strength
relative to the object
            (qed)

Who lifts anvils
these days (?) who
has really ever lifted
            an anvil (?)

IV (*Speed*)

Show the speed
of a quick act
write what speed
is

Is speed quick
wit uninter
rupted force
of example

Watch a fast train
zip by explain
what the observer
experiences

Is beyond speed
incomprehensible
like an unknown
gas

STRING QUARTET #6

(!)

, beware of abuse
of punctuation
for reasons strictly
poetic,

. stop at the start
here ends the frame
less which as we
all know…

¿ (question asked
in Spanish) ? the
first ? must be
flipped

: leads to: lists:
replaces , and *and* (some
times) acquainted with
grief

STRING QUARTET #7

I (*Delighted*)

Delighted Madame
delighted small birds
the sky really perfect
delighted

Small birds fly away
the sky is perfect really
delighted Madame
delighted

Delighted the sky really
delighted delighted really
Madame the small birds
        really

                    The sky Madame birds
                    small really small fly
                    away delighted perfect
                            really

II (*March*)

The left right left / of
the soldier's war
/ march gone
haywire

Tangled in the
li / nes shoes
wishing / to be
bare feet

The road spills its
kilo / meters en
slav / ing half
    the country

        Marchers take a
        bre / ak before head
        ing / north toward the
            unknown

III (*Slowing down*)

Meaning makes sense
senseless on this lasting
day of triumph
really

Nothing indispensable
note the casual air
of he who aspires
to the moment

The act the eye the instant
caught in a thick net
letting slip the instant
        the act the eye

                                 At least two times a day
                                 our gestures go through
                                 the daily gymnastics
                                     of slowing down

IV (*End*)

In the growing distance
a light flickers so
ftly *fails to*
shine

The *journey* fails
to show to say to
indicate what's left
to be traveled

No show no spectacle
only the dot along
the line little by little
      fading away

                There where the ground
                dips looks as if it *could*
                be the entrance to a
                      mine

ABOUT THE AUTHOR

Frédéric Forte has published 17 collections in the past ten years, each focused on a specific concept, often structural, and at times thematic. He became a member of the well-known Oulipo (Workshop of Potential Literature) in 2005, and teaches and does residencies throughout France. He lives in Paris, where (among many other things) he runs the blog poète-public.

ABOUT THE TRANSLATOR

Matthew B. Smith lives in Oakland. He has translated three works by the Belgian writer Jean-Philippe Toussaint and is completing a dissertation on contemporary French and American poetry at UC Berkeley.

This is the thirteenth title in the La Presse series
of contemporary French poetry in translation.
The series is edited by Cole Swensen, and this
edition is designed by Shari DeGraw.
Seven String Quartets is composed in
Adobe Jenson.

La Presse Poetry

TITLES IN PRINT

Theory of Prepositions
Claude Royet-Journoud
translated by Keith Waldrop

Wolftrot
Marie Borel
translated by Sarah Riggs & Omar Berrada

Heliotropes
Ryoko Sekiguchi
translated by Sarah O'Brien

Exchanges on Light
Jacques Roubaud
translated by Eleni Sikelianos

It
Dominique Fourcade
translated by Peter Consenstein

Conditions of Light
Emmanuel Hocquard
translated by Jean-Jacques Poucel

The Whole of Poetry is Preposition
Claude Royet-Journoud
translated by Keith Waldrop

A Woman with Several Lives
Jean Daive
translated by Norma Cole

Flirt Formula
Anne Portugal
translated by Jean-Jacques Poucel

Night and Day
Pierre Alferi
translated by Kate Campbell

Present Participle
Oscarine Bosquet
translated by Sarah Riggs and
Ellen LeBlond-Schrader

The L Notebook
Sabine Macher
translated by Eleni Sikelianos

Seven String Quartets
Frédéric Forte
translated by Matthew B. Smith